Bigg
Th

of Prayer

NELINE RACHEL
WOOLEY

EXECPT AS A CHILD PUBLISHING

Encourage Acclaim Restore

[1]

Bigger Than A Beetle: The Power of Prayer
published by Except As A Child Publishing LLC

Scripture quotations are from:

English Standard Version (ESV)
The Holy Bible, English Standard Version Copyright © 2001 by Crossway Bibles, a publishing ministry of Good News Publishers.

Also quoted:

International Children's Bible (ICB)
The Holy Bible, International Children's Bible® Copyright© 1986, 1988, 1999, 2015 by Tommy Nelson™, a division of Thomas Nelson. Used by permission.

New International Version (NIV)
Scriptures taken from Holy Bible, New International Version®, NIV® Copyright ©1973, 1978, 1984, 2011 by Biblica, Inc.® Used by permission. All rights reserved worldwide.

New King James Version (NKJV)
Scriptures taken from the New King James Version®. Copyright © 1982 by Thomas Nelson. Used by permission. All rights reserved.

Microsoft Office Clip Art used with permission from Microsoft

For information:
Except As A Child Publishing, LLC
PO BOX 68538
Indianapolis, IN 46268

Copyright © 2016 by Neline R Wooley

Printed in the United States of America

ISBN   978-0-692-64748-6

Table of Contents

Except As a Child…

This book is dedicated to my two grandsons
Andre Mykel Pipkin, Jr.
Nathan Elijah Pipkin

May God continue to guide you as you discover His amazing grace and mercy through the love of Jesus Christ.

Thank you to my daughter, Natalie, and my son-in-law, Andre Sr., for allowing me to share their parenting gifts and insight

Thank you to my son, Forrest, and my daughter, Melynda, for your love, prayers and support throughout this process

Thank you to my cousin Jennifer for stepping out and reaching back.

I love you!

[4]

Message from the Author

God is amazing! I know that doesn't sound profound or new, but these days have a need to say it out loud just to remind myself that He truly is.

The mystery and wonder that surrounds true worship is indeed breathtaking. For me, it is the *simplicity* of God's love through the shed blood of Jesus Christ that holds my attention.

I am so thankful every day for God's gifts of childlike, joyful insights on how to serve Him and show love to one another. Some will surely say it's because I am in that *#Grandma phase*. I choose to believe it's because God wants to emphasize, underline, and stick a pin in the fact that coming to Him and understanding His love through Jesus Christ is just that simple!

Life lessons through the eyes of my grandsons resonate in my spirit. I clearly see the beauty, patience, kindness, love, and faithfulness of God through the innocence of these children.

"Except as a child..."

Matthew 18:3 reminds us that we are to approach our relationship with God with complete humility, wide-eyed wonder, willingness to please, learn and grow—with the excitement and trust of a child. If we choose otherwise we will not complete the journey. We will not make it into His kingdom.

It is my hope that as you read and share this book with *all of the children* in your life, you will allow God to *open your eyes*. Take a look around! Simple messages and reminders of His love and grace surround *you*—everyday.

Matthew 28:20 (KJV)

Teaching them to observe all things whatsoever I have commanded you: and lo, I am with you always, even unto the end of the world. Amen.

Bigger than a Beetle
The power of prayer

Let's begin by saying I think bugs are
cool!

I have books all about them. One of my very
best favorite books is all about bug facts.

I hunt BUGS outside. I can even spot the tiniest bugs anywhere if they try to get into my house!

I know every move Spider-Man has ever made, plus a few I created myself.

But, today—today, I met my match!

I had a great day in First Grade even though I got off to a grumpy start this

 morning. Mom was on my case from the moment my feet hit the floor.

OK, yes. I may have been moving a little slowly and being what my parents call *uncooperative*, but we can talk about that another time.

Back to today…

I was in the back seat thinking about how much fun I had at recess when

Out of nowhere!

The biggest black beetle I had ever seen was on my pants leg!!

Kind of like this one.

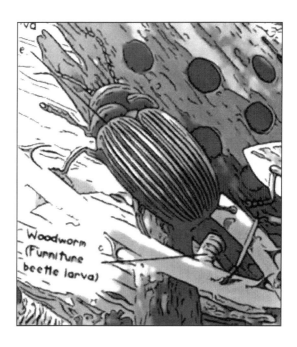

He was just sitting there with his hands in the air just staring directly right in my face!
You may as well say…

That bug was in my lap!

I screamed.

I yelled for my mom who was in the front seat driving. **And I cried.**

Yes! I cried like I didn't know I was six years old.

I was so afraid!

Oh, I forgot to tell you. I really, really do not like little spiders, flying insects and huge, scary, creepy, crawling bugs next to me—especially if I did not invite them!

I couldn't stop screaming, yelling and crying. Above all my noise, I heard my mom's voice.

"Andre, you will be all right," she said. "Pray to God."

"He will not let *anything* happen to you."

[11]

Mom called to me, "Andre, trust me."

"Listen to me."

"Pray to God."

So I did.
I prayed and prayed and prayed.

I prayed loudly!

I cried and prayed and cried and prayed.

Mom kept talking.

"Ask God to make the bug keep still," she said.

I did just that!
I didn't stop.
I couldn't stop.

Right in the middle of everything Mom says, "God is listening to you, Andre."

"He wants you and your brother to be safe."

"God wants you to trust Him and trust your mom and dad."

"God hears you when you humble yourself and pray to him with a sincere heart."

My mom **promised** that she would stop the car as soon as she could do it safely.

It took forever!
But I didn't stop praying!

"Help me, God.   Please help me!"

All of a sudden, Mom began to drive the car over to the Starbucks® coffee shop parking lot, and then …

That B I G scary bug started
moving down my pants leg!

I cried out to God and Mom even louder,
"Mom, it's moving!" I yelled.

My mom calmly said, "Andre, it only
moved because God knows we are about
to stop."

And we did!

Mom got out of the driver's seat and very carefully helped me out of my seat.

But, that bug wouldn't let go.

Mom said, "Stomp your foot, Andre." "Stomp your foot!"

So I did.

And that bug flew straight up into the sky. Right back where he came from!

[16]

I was still crying, but now I was thanking God and my Mom for taking care of all of us. I asked Mom how the beetle got in the car.

Mom said, "He either came from the window or the door."

"No," I said. "God put him right in my lap to teach me a lesson."

"To teach me how to trust Him more."

" Really trust Him!"

Then my little brother Nathan said something funny and we all laughed.

I thank God and Mom and Dad for teaching me how to trust and pray.

This is not a story. It is true! Amen.

Words to Remember

Faith   Trust   Pray   Humble
Obedient   Uncooperative

Dear Father in Heaven, please help me to trust you more. Your Word says you will be with me all the time. Just knowing that gives me peace in my heart.

Amen.

The Lord's Prayer

Matthew 6:9-13

International Children's Bible (ICB)

[9] So when you pray, you should pray like this:

'Our Father in heaven,
we pray that your name will always be kept holy.
[10] We pray that your kingdom will come.
We pray that what you want will be done,
 here on earth as it is in heaven.
[11] Give us the food we need for each day.
[12] Forgive the sins we have done,
 just as we have forgiven those who did wrong to us.
[13] And do not cause us to be tested;
but save us from the Evil One.'
 [The kingdom, the power, and the glory are yours forever. Amen.]

.

[22]

I can do it!

Self Correction

What a day! I am so glad to be home.

Mom reminded me to change out of my school clothes. Believe me she didn't have to tell me twice!

I was ready to get out of those *"beetle pants"*. So I did—with lightening speed!

I told Mom that I had a talk with one of the guys at my school last week.   I told him that he needed to pray a little more.

This guy is…well let's just say, if something is going on not so good in my first grade class, you can count on ***this guy*** being right in the middle.

When I mention any trouble at school, Dad, Mom and Grandma always remind me to pray to God about it. I think I will tell God about the guys in my classroom. Especially about how they play basketball and checkers!

I was so glad to be home from school. I came down the stairs super fast.

I was just about to run down the hall, when I quickly remembered Rule #5

Rule 5: "No running in the house".

It was like I had invisible brakes on my feet.

"Look, Mom!", I said.

Standing tall like a soldier I walked slowly and carefully into the kitchen. "Mom, I remembered Rule #5 without you reminding me!"

"I can do the right thing all by myself!"

Mom just smiled!

I can do all things through Christ because he gives me strength. Philippians 4:13 (ICB)

Read, Set, Go...
This is War!

Uh, oh—I could tell this was going to be a serious day!

Mom just announced she was going to have a talk with my teacher. She had warned me several times that she was going to tell Mrs. D. all about my at-home behavior.

Just the thought of that discussion gives me the heebie-jebbies. Every time Mom says anything about telling my teacher **ANYTHING**—I beg, I plead and I promise. "No, no, no, Mom!!!"

I do not want my good reputation at school to be spoiled by Mom's play-by-play report on some of my very *uncooperative* actions at home.

But, today, Mom reached her limit!

Let me be honest here. Some days I just wake up and don't seem to want to listen. I can't explain it! It's like someone pulled a plug while I was sleeping.

But, back to today's situation…

Yesterday, I had to be out of school to go to the dentist, so my teacher saved the class work I missed and gave it to me for homework. She said I didn't have to bring it all back until Friday, but it was a lot!

1…2…3… Four pages!!!

Don't get me wrong. I love homework.

Really! I do!!

100's make me extremely happy.

But just not today!

Well, I really tried to get over it, but all I could think about was how I didn't want to do all of this work. I was getting *frustrated*.

That's my favorite description of how I feel when I begin to get angry inside and really don't know why.

First I stop listening. Then I make sounds like a giant bear, but really softly so no one can hear me.

GRRRRR GRRRR GRRRRR

Then, everything kind of gets out of control…

Today was that kind of day!

School seemed extra long and now all that homework came out of nowhere.

I just wanted to go home and play with my brother….Spider Man, Ninja Turtles,

eat snacks, spin around like an airplane
…anything but homework!!

When we got home, the first thing Mom
said was—

"Andre, please change out of your school clothes and let's get to some of this homework before dinner."

I changed very slowly and I came down stairs with my grumpiest face. It's the face I use when I want everyone to know—as soon as they see me—I have a lot on my mind.

Somehow, it didn't work! I practiced in the mirror, but Mom didn't even look. She had my snack ready and that homework was sitting there waiting on me.

"You can do it Andre," she said. *"Just read the directions and get to it. I'll check your work."*

"But Mom," I moaned. "It's too much!"

Mom just repeated what she said earlier.

"Andre, it's not even due until Friday. Please read your directions and I will check your work when you are finished."

So, I sat there and stared at the papers. My mind was totally blank, except for the thought that I did not want to do my work.

Fifteen minutes later…

Mom came over to the homework table to check on me. *"Andre, what's the problem?"* she asked.

Out of nowhere I heard myself loudly reply,

"Mom, YOU are not my teacher!"

I don't know where that voice came from. My Mom looked very, very disappointed.

I knew there was a timeout, fireworks, or something coming my way.

I was prepared to take whatever was going to happen next, just as long as I didn't have to do this awful homework!

Instead, Mom calmly talked to me about how important it was to do my homework and *blah, blah, blah*...I really don't know what she said because I wasn't listening.

Then Mom raised her voice and told me to march right up to my room *to think* about what I was going to do.

So I slowly went upstairs.

I went right to my room with my LEGO® collection, my drums, my dinosaurs, and my super hero action figures.

And, I just sat on my bed.

I could hear Mom, Dad, and my little brother having a great time downstairs.

That's where I wanted to be—having fun. Not doing homework!!

Mom called me from all the way downstairs, in that *creepy* calm Mom voice…

"So, *Andre*, what have you decided?"

I hurried downstairs, stood up straight and tall and proudly announced…

"I am NOT going to do my work!"

Everyone got quiet. Even my little brother!

Everyone was looking at me, but no one said anything.

Finally, Mom said, "That's fine. It's your choice!"

I was just about to jump for joy, when I heard the next sentence, loud and clear.

"Go upstairs and brush your teeth. It's time to get ready for bed."

What! My plan didn't work!!!

Oh, let me take a moment here to tell you about tooth brushing.

I don't know…. It's just another thing that I don't really like.

When I don't like to do something, I do it very slowly. Because, I don't like it!

When I take too much time brushing my teeth *(or in this case not brushing my teeth)* Mom or Dad help me and then I feel like a little kid.

I turn my head a thousand times or close my mouth as long as I can. It always ends up the same— clean teeth and we're all frustrated.

I finally told my parents that it was the bubbles. Yes, the bubbles. I just don't like all those bubbles in my mouth!

So what did they do? Mom and Dad went out the next day and got toothpaste without bubbles!!!

So, now it's time to brush my teeth. I really don't care about this new no-bubble toothpaste. I just don't want to brush my teeth. I am very *frustrated,* again!

Nothing is going my way today and now I am MAD!

All I can do is just stand here and shout out to everyone….

"I Am Mad!"

Uh, oh! By the look on my Mom's face, she wasn't so happy either.

"Enough is enough!" she said in a very loud voice.

Mom took me by my hand and marched  me right to her bedroom.

And, there it was. Right in front of me—

Mom and Dad's prayer closet?

Yes, it's their prayer closet all right.

Sometimes Mom calls it her "**War Room**", but I don't know what that's about. Mom doesn't know much about the *real* Ninja Turtle fighting stuff.

That's my territory!

Hmmm… No windows. No doors.

Just prayers! Prayers my Mom and Dad wrote on different sized papers taped to the wall. There is a bible, pictures of our family, a couple of pillows, and now…

Mom and me!

Mom held my hand as she got down on her knees and started to pray. Not quietly, but very, very loudly to God.

Oh, No! Now what? It sounds like—

Mom is telling on ME directly to God!

Mom told God that she was *absolutely* done struggling for peace in our home.

She said something about rebuking Satan. *(That's the evil spirit that is always trying to fight against God).* Mom began to cry out loud to God. Lots of tears were coming down her face really fast.

She was asking God to change *my* heart, to change *my* mind, to help me be the child who would show God how much I loved Him by simply obeying my parents!

It's like I was right beside Mom, but at the same time she forgot I was there.

Mom was only talking to God!

Then something happened.

I could feel tears coming down MY face, too. I was on my knees next to Mom.

I lifted both my hands in the air and began to talk to God myself.

"God, I don't want to do this anymore."

"I hate all the bad stuff I have done."

"Why did I do this?"

"Why did I do this?"

Mom looked over at me and said very quietly, "The Holy Spirit can help you, Andre."

"You cannot be good all by yourself."

"No one can. God has a helper on the inside of you to be with you always."

"Andre, would you like salvation (God's saving love) through Jesus Christ?"

"Would you like to be saved?"

Right then, Mom reminded me how we talked about God's only son, Jesus Christ and how Jesus died for our sins and how after God raised Him from the tomb, God sent the Holy Spirit to help us make right decisions.

"Forgive yourself, Andre. Follow Jesus. Followers don't look back, they look forward."

What matters is that you care right there in your heart," Mom said softly.

Then my mom read scriptures to me from the Holy Bible about a man named Saul and how the Lord changed him from doing bad things and renamed him Paul.

And then Mom said, "God can change you, Andre. Do you want to be saved?"

"Yes! Yes!" I said very loudly.

"Yes, I want to be saved!"

"I love you guys so much."

"I don't want to hurt you!"

Now, Mom was giving me a big hug.

"Repent and walk in your salvation, Andre!" Mom said quietly.

That means stop doing the wrong things and start doing what's right. Mom explained that part to me, too.

I was crying and Mom was crying. She just kept saying over and over...

"You are forgiven. You <u>ARE</u> forgiven!"

Right then and there I started smiling. I couldn't help it. Tears were everywhere. All over my face and I just kept smiling.

I could hear myself saying . . .

"I am just so HAPPY!"

"I can't explain it!"

"It's crazy."

"Nothing is wrong!"

"I got saved!"

"I am not sad, but every time I smile tears keep coming out!"

"Look, Mom!" I said showing her my face.

"Happy Smile….Tears come down."

"Happy Smile…Tears come down!"

Mom held me close and whispered, *"Andre, always remember, God always provides a way out."*

When I woke up the next morning,

I couldn't wait to tell Mom, Dad, and my brother that I was still very, very happy inside!

Amen.

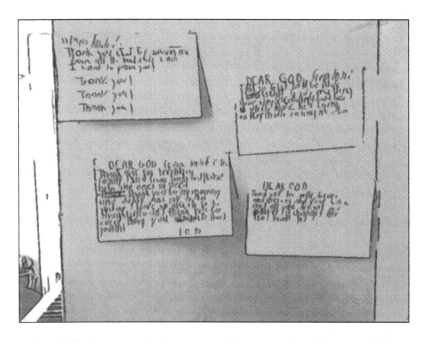

A child saved is a soul saved, plus a life.

Church of God in Christ International
Sunday School Motto

Andre's Prayers

December 9, 2015
Thank you God for saving me from all the bad stuff I did. I want to praise you.
Thank you
Thank you
Thank you

Dear God from Andre
I am so glad to be alive
I want to say one thing
Three simple words
God is not dead
He's living on the inside
Roaring like a lion

Dear God
Thank you for your Grace and Mercy and Your Love and all you did.
Your power it changes me
So I thank you

January 12, 2016
Dear God from Andre P Jr.
Thank you for keeping my family safe from harm and please help the ones in need. Thank you for my mommy and daddy and my brother and me. I have so much to be thankful for and thank you for everything you made. Thank you!!!

Salvation Is Not *Perfection*

There are definitely "morning people" and those that are simply "not-morning people"…

> Believe me. I understand.
> I am a #morningperson!

I love the sunshine, the birds, my quiet time, the peace, and the energy of mornings.

> NONE of my children are
> #morningpeople!

My grandson, Andre Jr., is NOT a morning person!!

Maybe if his school would begin at noon and every Saturday and Sunday, he could sleep in—life would be A-OK! (the "A" is for Andre)

That's so funny to me—well everything
is funny to me today (LOL)—
      "A" is for Andre and
      "A" is also for Alvin.

      Yes, the chipmunk!

These two guys are very similar.
Trust me!

If you substitute "Andre" for "Alvin" in the movies and books, you wouldn't be too far off, if you are trying to figure out who Andre Jr. is.

Andre's mom just shared another wonderful glimpse into *the life and times of Andre, Jr.*

Shall we....

How your morning starts off can sometimes set the path for the whole, entire day.

Not being a morning person, Andre Jr. is best left alone in the morning until God wakes him up thoroughly—in the name of Jesus!

Since Andre is six years old, and in the First Grade, God has graciously appointed the *"getting Andre Jr. up"* ritual to Mom and Dad.

"Get up, Andre."

"It's time to get ready for school, Andre."

"Brush your teeth, Andre."

"Hurry, Andre. You are going to miss breakfast."

"Andre."
"Andre!"
"A N D R E!!!"

If I didn't know better, I would say
Andre just likes to hear the sound of his
name.

Mom went about the regular routine
because today was also a school day and
a field trip day for Nathan, Andre's little
brother.

A trip to Earth Fare! Can't be late!! The
field trip bus is always on time!!!

When Mom came back to check on
Andre *(because she always does),*
nothing had been accomplished.

No washing up.
No brushing teeth.

[53]

And, Andre's school clothes were still neatly folded at the end of his bed.

Everything was waiting for Mr. Droopy Pajamas (Andre Jr.).

"Times up, Andre"
"Get your clothes on. We have to go!",
warned mom.

"But Mom," whined Andre.

"No sir! No time for anything else,"
replied Mom.

FINALLY Andre put on his school clothes, hurried downstairs to get his lunch box, and to his surprise—

No lunch!

Yes, that's right. No lunch in his Ninja Turtle lunch box. Instead Mom had three dollars ($3.00) from Andre's bank all ready for him in a special envelope.

Andre was going to have to eat

SCHOOL LUNCH!!

"Aw, Man!" he groaned.

You see, school lunch is not really one of Andre's favorite things, especially when he has to use his own savings to pay for it.

Andre immediately pledged not to eat it. No, Sir. No way. No how! No school lunch for this guy.

Mom reminded Andre how that would be wasting food that other children may really need or want.

It was hard to imagine anyone wanting school lunch, but Andre knew Mom was right.

Mom kept it moving and offered Andre a juice box to go with his quick breakfast.

"I want the other juice," he replied as he passed the box over to his brother.

"Andre, this is the same juice we have had all week," Mom said.

"But, Mom. Dad bought the *other* juice for me when we went to the store. It's got to be in there."

Now, Mom was getting frustrated. Very frustrated. *(That's Andre's favorite word.)*

Just then, Dad stepped into the kitchen. "Andre, I remember you saying that you <u>did not</u> want the new flavor, so I didn't get it."

"Aw, Man! I did say that, but I still just wanted to try it," Andre said a little disappointed.

Mom kept it moving—because that's what Mom does.

As Andre began to put on his coat and hat, he remembered something else.

He did not wash his face. He did not brush his teeth.

And he wasn't quite sure if he even changed his underwear!

What! This is just not going to work!!

"No, Sir." said Mom. "Time is up. We have to go!"

"Maybe if your friends smell a little something different about you today, maybe you can share your morning routine with them."

Andre did not think Mom was funny. No time for choices now. In fact, time was really up. The family car was loading for school drop offs.

When everyone was safely buckled in and settled, Mom turned down the radio so both boys could clearly hear every word she was about to say.

Andre leaned his head back against his seat. This was going to be a *consequence* talk! Andre could recognize it anywhere.

Whenever Mom doesn't like how the boys are conducting themselves, the radio goes silent and Mom presents the *On the Way to Anywhere* lesson for the day at the first opportunity!

"Respect, guys!" she said. "That is a very important part of this life."

"Andre, it is so wonderful that God has shown His love and mercy and accepted you as His child."

"I am so thankful for the positive, great changes in your attitude and behavior."

"But, what I also know is that Satan is not happy with all these changes. Satan wants to convince you and others around you that you do not belong to God."

"Guys, Satan is a liar."

"Yes! Your Mom just said it!!"

"Satan is a liar. In fact the Holy Bible tells us that he is the Father of Lies."

"I need both you guys to show respect to your parents by just obeying. That is actually one of God's commandments with a special promise just for you."

Ephesians 6:1-3 (NIV)

Children, obey your parents in the Lord, for this is right. [2] "Honor your father and mother"—which is the first commandment with a promise— [3] "so that it may go well with you and that you may enjoy long life on the earth."

"Listen and obey."

"Andre, I do believe with all my heart that you are saved by the grace of God, and I do know how much you love Jesus Christ and learning more about His works and His love for you."

"God's Word gives me and Dad no option but to give both of you guys complete directions on how to be great young men."

"God corrects adults when we get off focus and out of favor with Him. God expects loving parents to do the same for children under their care. Daddy and I love you so much!"

"God's Word tells us that obedience is better than all the other gifts we may want to give Him. God reminds us that if we truly love Him—I mean really, really love Him, we will obey."

If you love Me, you will keep My commandments. John 14:15 (NIV)

"Andre, you have accepted Jesus Christ as your Savior and you have accepted the Holy Spirit into your heart. Always remember the power you have on your side. Good wins every time!   Allow the Holy Spirit to help you make the right choices."

When the family van arrived at Andre's school, Andre could feel that *happy feeling* from the Holy Spirit right inside his heart again, just like before!

"We are here, Andre," Mom said. "Get your backpack together." "Have a great day. I love you!"

Andre understood everything Mom was saying. Just like all of Mom's consequence talks it made him so happy to know Mom and Dad cared.

Now, Andre wanted just a little more time with Mom and his little brother, Nathan, before he started his day.

So, he asked one more little question as he collected his things.

"Mom, will you come in to Chapel and pray with me today?"
"Please, please—."

And she did!
Andre already had a prayer in his heart.

Thank you, God, for being in my life and loving me when I'm feeling less than 100%.

And, I'm brushing my teeth as soon as I get home! Amen.

Hidden Treasures

Hi! My name is Nathan. I am Andre's little brother. I am 3 years old, well really 3½.

My family is fun and my brother is a good teacher. All I have to do is watch! It is kind of like watching a movie, but you are really inside the TV with it.

Andre learns all the hard lessons for both of us. I just listen and watch, while Mommy helps him get it right.

Life is pretty easy, breezy—so far!

One special thing you can know about me is that I really like to eat. That works great because Mommy is the best cooker in the whole world!

Sometimes, Mommy lets me and my brother help in the kitchen.

We help make cupcakes, cookies, pizzas and we even help mix pancakes too.

My brother and I have our own kitchen. It is red and it's called a "Cook and Grow" Kitchen.

I really like making dinners in my own kitchen. Sometimes I use blocks, LEGO® pieces or sometimes puzzles when I cook. Everyone likes everything I make even though it's just pretend food.

Today, Mommy is making Beef Stew. Mommy said this will be a good dinner with lots of vegetables to help make me big and strong.

Early this morning Mommy put all the ingredients (that's the stuff that goes together to make Mommy's dinner so yummy) on the counter.

Mommy chopped onions and potatoes. Then she chopped up the red meat (Mommy says that's beef) and placed it in a large bowl of white powdery stuff.

Next, Mommy put the meat in a very hot pan to make the meat turn brown.

Mommy put the pepper, and the salt and the other spicy things on the counter too. Then, Mommy announced that we were ready to put the beef stew together!

Our big kitchen was beginning to smell great and my tummy was getting hungry.

I was counting the ingredients
One—Two—Three—Four…

When all of a sudden, Mommy said,
"Oh, no! I don't have any carrots!!"

That was OK with me because carrots are vegetables, and vegetables <u>are not</u> my favorite things to eat.

Mommy was moving fast. She helped me with my jacket and my shoes. Then Mommy put on her coat and walked us both out to the garage.

Right as we were about to get me in my car seat, Mommy stopped. "Wait a minute", she said out loud.

"What is it, Mommy?" I said. "Do you want Bruce to go with us?"

 Bruce is our family dog. I just wanted to see if I could make Mommy laugh.

And I did!

"No!" she said. "I forgot something very important."

Mommy took us both back into the house. After Mommy put the car keys on the table, we went outside to the backyard.

What could it be? Maybe Mommy needed to play basketball first or just give me a push in the swing before we go to the store. That would be great!

When we got outside, Mommy took me right over to Daddy's vegetable garden.

I look at it every day! Daddy's garden has tomatoes and onions and peppers. He even has a big pot with potatoes growing right inside.

"Guess what, Nathan!" Mommy said.

"Guess what Daddy has growing right over there."

"Strawberries!" I said jumping up and down. "I love Strawberries!!"

"No, Nathan!" Mommy was laughing again.

"Daddy has carrots in his garden. Carrots for our beef stew."

"God has provided just what I needed to make a really good dinner for our family."

"We do not have to rush to the store."

"We do not have to spend any money."

"All we needed to do was to look in our own backyard!"

"I am thankful to God for His Holy Spirit reminding us that He will provide all of our needs," Mommy said.

Mommy was very happy! We went right over to Daddy's garden and pulled and tugged at the little green leaves growing in a row. After a few tugs—out popped a carrot and another and another, until Mommy had all the carrots she needed for dinner.

Mommy talked with me about God's blessings and asked me to always pray and ask God to show me where to find His hidden treasures.

Thank you, God, for dinner. But, I still do not like carrots that much—on my plate. Maybe Mommy will make smoothies!

Amen!

Every good action and every perfect gift is from God. These good gifts come down from the Creator of the sun, moon, and stars. God does not change like their shifting shadows.

James 1:17 (ICB)

10 Bible Verses for Children

1. In the beginning, God created the heavens and the earth. **Genesis 1:1** (ESV)

2. Every word of God proves true. **Proverbs 30:5** (ESV)

3. Children obey your parents in the Lord, for this is right. **Ephesians 6:1** (ESV)

4. Without faith no one can please God. Anyone who comes to God must believe that he is real and that he rewards those who truly want to find him. **Hebrews 11:6** (ICB)

5. Do not be afraid for I am with you. **Isaiah 43:5** (ESV)

6. Whatever you do, do everything for the glory of God. **1 Corinthians 10:31** (ESV)

7. I praise you God, for I am fearfully and wonderfully made. **Psalm 139:14** (ESV)

8. Love the LORD your God with all your heart and with all your soul and with all your might. **Deuteronomy 6:5** (ESV)

9. Let no one despise you for your youth, but set the believers an example in speech, in conduct, in love, in faith, in purity. **1 Timothy 4:12** (ESV)

10. All your children will be taught by the Lord. And they will have much peace. **Isaiah 54:13** (ICS)

Salvation is for Children, too!

• **Pray:** Pray for your child by name! Ask God to prepare him/her to understand and receive the good news about Jesus and prepare you to effectively communicate with patience and love.

• **Share the Good News:** Use words and phrases your child can understand. Talk about the scriptures slowly enough to allow time for thinking and understanding.

a. "God wants you to become His child. Do you know why God wants you in His family?" Read 1 John 4:8 (NIV).

b. "You and I and every person in the world have done wrong things. The Bible word for doing wrong is 'sin.' What do you think should happen to us when we sin?" Read Romans 6:23 (NIV)

c. "God loves you so much, He sent His Son to die on the cross for your sin. Because Jesus never sinned, He is the only one who can take the punishment for our sin."
Read 1 Corinthians 15:3; 1 John 4:14.(NIV)

d. "Are you sorry for your sin? Tell God that you are. Do you believe Jesus died to take the punishment for your sin? If you tell God you are sorry for your sin and tell Him you do believe and accept Jesus sacrificing His life on the cross to take away your sin; God is faithful to forgive your sin." Read John 1:12.(NIV)

e. "The Bible says that when you believe in Jesus, God's Son, you receive God's gift of eternal life. This gift makes you a child of God. This means God is with you now and forever." Read John 3:16 (NIV)

The idea of being a child of God is perhaps the simplest example the New Testament provides.

• **Talk with your child:** Talking about salvation one-on-one opens up the opportunity to ask and answer questions. Ask questions that need more than a simple "yes" or "no" answers or a replay with of memorized words. Ask "what-do-you-think?" kinds of questions such as:

"Why do you think it's important to...?"

"What are some things you really like about Jesus?"

"Why do you think that Jesus had to die because of wrong things you and I have done?"

"What difference do you think it makes for a person to be forgiven?"

Answers to these open questions will help you learn how much your child understands.

• **Give time to think and pray:**   It is important to encourage your child to think and pray about what you have said before making a response. Also allow time for quiet thinking about the questions you ask.

• **Offer opportunities without pressure:** A good way to guard against answering for your child's is to simply pause often and ask, "Would you like to hear more about this now or at another time?"

Loving acceptance is so important, even when your child is not completely focused on the topic of salvation through Jesus Christ. Your personal walk and daily commitment to showing God's love is the best gift you can share. Plant and water, God will do the rest!

Matthew 19:14 (NIV)
Jesus said, "Let the **little children** come to me, and do not hinder them, for the kingdom of heaven belongs to such as these."